The Tw....

Natalie Carter

*"Nothing has brought us more joy than sharing our lives with a breed
of dog who can be so serious and so stupid all in the same breath"*
- N Carter

ISBN-10: 1499715978
ISBN-13: 978-1499715972

CONTENTS

ACKNOWLEDGMENTS

I would like to thank my husband, Laurence, for encouraging the freedom to decide which career I wanted to pursue in life.

Had I not become a dog walker when I did, I would not have had the time to work on this book and spend each special day with the twins and get to enjoy their personalities. I would also like to thank John & Philomena Warriner, both who which, upon their visit to us in the US in 2014, took the time to read through my stories and provide helpful feedback.

DEDICATIONS

I am dedicating this book to my late grandmother.
Rene Carter.

The Choosing

It was a long time before both myself and my husband, Laurence, were ready to adopt a dog into our life, but the perfect opportunity arrived when Laurence took on a job working night shifts. I was very bored in the evenings and felt very vulnerable being left alone. So we had a little chat and talked about dog breeds we liked. Instantly he said "I really like Dobermanns", to this day I have no idea why he said that or where he had even seen a Dobermann before, he'd never owned a dog let alone a large breed. In my family I grew up with an Irish Setter, a Jack Russell and a rescue mixed Miniature Pincher.

I wasn't that fussed about a Dobermann, at the time I still very much wanted a Dalmatian, but Laurence insisted on emailing me daily pictures of Dobermann puppies and handsome adult dogs. So from then I decided to buy a couple of books and do some researching. In fact I bought quite a lot of books, some old, some new, some borrowed and yes, one is blue. After lots of reading we decided to go and look at some rescue centres.

The first rescue centre I went too sat us down and had me fill in three A4 pages of information, right at the end it asked about our home. At the time we were living in a 2 bedroom first floor maisonette with shared gardens, surrounded by countryside and farmer fields in every direction. Our village only had one post office and one fuel station it was so small. The rescue centre reviewed our form and pulled us up on our communal gardens. She advised us that because the garden was not fully enclosed we could not have a dog from their rescue centre.

Deflated, we went to another rescue centre where my parents had rescued their miniature pincher and my ferrets from. When we arrived the man in front of us was handing in a female Dobermann, around 3 years of age, she was gorgeous and I instantly liked her; I also considered it a sign. We spoke to the receptionist and explained the dog being handed over was exactly what we were after but she still insisted on us filling out some more forms. So we sat down for another half hour, took them back to the desk to be told that because we had shared gardens we could not adopt a dog from their rescue.

The next day I called a reputable Dobermann rehoming group, and I spoke with the lady there for a good hour, only to be told at the end of the conversation that she would never re-home a Dobermann to me because I didn't have experience of Dobermanns. I couldn't help but think how ironic that was - if I couldn't get hold of a Dobermann how on earth was I to get experience!

It was the next day Laurence said to me that with a rescue Dobermann he would have been concerned if anything happened to me whilst he was working nights, as they were a powerful breed and if I were to be challenged he would worry I would get hurt. So from that moment we decided to go on the hunt for a puppy.

We eventually found a breeder over in Marlborough, UK who had two female pups left. We were sat in the lounge with these two leggy pups racing about bowling eachother over. We had no idea which one to pick, I had researched some tests that you can do to pups to make sure you are getting a submissive and alert one, so we clapped, we rolled them on their backs, we levitated them to see if they struggled and they both gave the same response.

So I did what any responsible person would do. I picked the one with a funny looking bald patch on her head.

The Arrival 2006

We collected Roxy in the evening, armed with wet wipes, towels and box. But none of it was needed as she fell asleep on my lap all the way home. When we arrived home we plonked her down in the middle of the lounge and let the cat come down from the shelf in her own time. Eventually she came down took one sniff of Roxy and swiped her across the nose.

Roxy, now a bit scared, proceeded to squeeze through the baby gate, trot off down the hall and have a nice big poo on the landing…. Grrreaaaattt.

Then if I'm honest for the next 2-3 weeks she was mostly asleep!

She grew quite rapidly and by the time she was 4 months old she'd started to look like a giraffe. I was always amused at how, even by this point, we were already getting the people crossing the road to avoid us, and picking up their smaller dogs in case 'the big scary Dobermann' ate it!

Roxy was a great puppy, we had a few issues with the ol' toilet training but then again, we knew it wasn't going to be easy living in a first floor maisonette. I still have images of one night Laurence, upon seeing Roxy start to wee on the carpet, lifted her up and ran down the stairs, all the while she was still weeing, the walls were a lovely shade of yellow!

But because this problem, became, well, such a problem, we decided to invest in a doggie door bell. The logic seemed quite simple, there was a button on the floor and when Roxy needed to go out for a wee she just pushed the button with her paw, the alarm would woof a few times and then we'd take her outside. Someone neglected to warn me however, that Roxy would use this, just because she wanted to go out, not because she needed a wee.

One evening, Roxy pushed the button, I rushed her down the stairs, no wee, so I took her back up, took the lead off and she jumped on the button again, so I rushed her back downstairs, still no wee. So I took her back up the stairs and with a huge grin on her face she promptly jumped on the button again, by this point I was exhausted and bored of the new game she had invented for herself. So I said no and walked off back into the lounge. It went quiet for a minute, then came the waft of dog poo. As I went back out into the hallway, sure enough a nice big poo right next to the sodding doggie door bell!!!

Needless to say the bell was packed up back into the box that night and lived out the rest of its life in the loft.

Roxy aged 2 months

The Moth

At around 4 months of age Roxy had established her sleeping place on Laurence's dressing robe which was often strewed in a mess on the floor. We had originally purchased a crate as the books had advised, but she was quite defiant not to be shut away, and unfortunately for us being in a maisonette and not having very co-operative neighbours we had no choice but to let her sleep in the bedroom.

The robe, over any expensive bed we purchased, was her sleeping place of choice. One particular night we had finally managed to persuade Roxy to sleep in her own bed (using our super-smart skills of simply putting the robe on her new bed!) We were both sitting up reading, when a moth flew past our line of sight and fluttered casually down towards puppy Roxy, it promptly landed upon her forehead which lead to the following almighty squeel, a panicked run across the bedroom, a gigantic leap onto our bed and under the duvet, shivering, hiding between Laurence and myself. The place where she then ended up sleeping every night for the following six months!

Roxy aged 4 months

The Attack

Roxy was only about six months old, when we were making the most of a beautiful sunny afternoon and sitting in the middle of our local field. A new neighbour also came down and joined us, Roxy was prancing around, a cute little 6 month old pup and the neighbour's old Jack Russell was milling about. The Russell owner produced some dog treats to give Roxy but unfortunately her Jack took offense to this and bit Roxy on the nose. I quickly took her home and put some pressure on the wound but thought nothing of it, accidents happen! But this is why, as many people ask, Roxy has always had a scar on her nose.

So I was surprised to hear a few weeks later that the owner of the Jack Russell wasn't speaking to me anymore. I had always waved, been polite, so I wasn't sure what was going on. Then the gossiping neighbourhood stepped in for me, I was told that someone had reported the attack to the local Dog Warden. I was surprised as it was nothing to do with anyone else nor were any persons there to witness the attack. And I was also upset as the Jack Russell owner obviously thought it was me that called the dog warden. However much to my surprise someone had been trying to blame the 'vicious' 6 month old Dobermann for the attack. This was my first encounter with breedist people.

Roxy aged 6 months

First experience of water

Roxy was about nine months old when we decided to take her on a week long trip to Scotland! What a wonderful week that was, I am still surprised by how dog friendly everyone was in Scotland and although it was a bit cold we made the most of each day. One day, we went to a shingle type beach and Laurence was jumping over all the big rocks down towards the sea. Now one thing Roxy loves to do, to this day, is rock climb, and she is actually very good at it. I've never seen a dog's paws spread into webs before but its pretty impressive and gives her a lot of grip whilst jumping from rock to rock.

So I was busy taking photos of my hubby down by the seaside, when in the corner of the camera I saw a little Dobie pup bounding at a fast pace towards him. Only she didn't stop and sure enough "splosh" straight into the sea, as I put the camera down to panic she quickly emerged in a dolphin style leap out of the ocean, and ungracefully jumped her way quickly back towards the safety of the beach, fortunately I captured it all on camera so it will be a reminder for a future me of exactly why Roxy doesn't like water anymore.

Roxy bounding out of the water in Scotland

The Cable Car

Also on our Scotland trip we decided to take a trip to Ben Nevis, but being both completely unhealthy and extremely unfit at the time we decided to take the cable car. What we didn't count on was that Roxy wasn't too keen on jumping into a moving lift. So after we missed three lifts, Laurence quickly picked a very gangly nine month old Roxy up and we both jumped onto the lift. She wasn't impressed at 1. being manhandled too quickly and 2. being on some sort of object that was moving and making a funny noise. I had never seen Roxy drool so much in 5 minutes and freeze into statue mode. But fortunately she was much happier on the way back down!

Roxy in the Cable Car

The man wearing a hat

So I am not really sure why, but whilst looking into different training things to do with a puppy we stumbled across ringcraft. Essentially, teaching your dog to stand still and look pretty. So we attended a few sessions at our local hall.

It was a nice class but didn't seem to make much sense to me, we just walked round in circles and some women came over and looked at the dogs faces, then we went home. Anyway, clearly after one lesson, I knew exactly what I was doing and entered Roxy into a big crufts-style Dog Show. I even went out and bought an expensive showing dog lead, convinced that this was a piece of cake and all I had to do was stand there.

We arrived at this show which was much bigger than I had expected. As our class was called up to show I put Roxy in her fancy new lead, Laurence wished me luck and we elegantly strode into the ring, however I was not aware that about fifty other dogs would also be in this class. To be fair I don't even remember what type of class I entered, but we were up against many different breeds. So Roxy got bored, she whined, pined to see her dad, she rolled about in the grass, she bugged every dog around us, to the annoyance of the ladies either side of me, when that didn't work she decided to yap slightly every now and again, just to let me know how extremely bored she was.

I was desperately trying everything, treats, ball, tricks, anything just to stop her messing about. Then finally we were called up, phew, we pranced over to the judge and I held Roxy's lead up like how I had seen every person in front of me do, but as this old chap in a very large wicker hat leant forward, Roxy decided he was the most terrifying person on earth. She leapt back in the air like I had just caught a wild coyote that was trying desperately to escape. Fortunately the chap seemed aware, not sure how, that this was her first show and just gave her a pat on the head and let me go on my merry way. What a disaster. So I was pleasantly surprised when the judge awarded Roxy a pink rosette that just said the word 'special' on it. That pretty much summed her up.

Our special Pink rosette

No more showing

I honestly can see why so many people are bitten by the bug to show their dogs. There is nothing nicer than some complete stranger telling you your dog looks good, and rosettes are an incentive to do better! So now I had this lovely pink Rosette, I wanted another one. A few months later we entered a similar show, this time I attended with my sister. And this time I was clever, I entered ALL of the classes. However we didn't plan on this being one of the hottest days of the year. So we spent most of our time waiting under trees, down by the lake getting prepared for our class.

Finally we were called up, I was super excited, wet-wiped Roxy down so she looked all pretty, had my expensive show collar and pranced into the ring, which happened to have zero shelter and the dogs were heating up very quickly. There was a lady walking round with a bucket of water offering it to the dogs, but I was very surprised they didn't at least split the group to save us standing there for hours. After what felt like an hour, but was probably 20 minutes I looked at my poor Dobermann, who was so hot she was just laid out on the floor panting, I decided to get out of the ring and find some more water. We saw a bunch of dogs playing near a tap that had been left on so I let Roxy off the lead and she ran over to join in, the ground below the tap quickly turned to mud and with three or four dogs jumping about in there, it quickly went everywhere, in fact within a few minutes my beautiful clean Black & Tan Dobermann was a "Covered in pure mud" Dobermann. But do you know what, I didn't care, she had a smile on her face that I wont forget, we never went back into the class and we didn't bother going to the rest of the classes entered.

Flyball anyone?

Having decided that showing probably wasn't Roxy forte. I heard that our local dog trainer was setting up a flyball class, I had not really seen a lot on the sport, so wasn't entirely sure what it was about other than what I had read. So we turned up and there was a fairly large group of people standing in the field.

Set up in the middle were a few low hurdles with someone the end of the hurdles to throw a tennis ball towards the dogs, all seemed quite fun. However I had failed to remember that as much as Roxy loves to chase and catch a ball, she is not so keen to bring it back.

In the instance a ball is ever thrown out of sight, in her case it's "out of sight, out of mind", if she didn't see a ball land, it never existed and ends up with me or Laurence traipsing through thorns and bushes to retrieve them. So with this knowledge in mind, I probably should have realised flyball wasn't the best sport for our Roxy. She jumped those hurdles like a pro, caught that ball with one fowl swoop and proceeded to gallop off into the distance, never once looking back, showing all those other dogs how great she was at being an expert thief. I spent the rest of the hour attempting and failing miserably to get that ball back.

Agility is better

When Roxy was just over a year old I decided to join a local agility club, of course like everyone else I had to go through a 3 month introduction plan, but was amazed when I was quickly picked to become a full time member of the club and attend weekly training sessions. Sometimes having an unusual breed has its advantages.

In the early months Roxy was showing real potential in agility, although it wasn't long until you could see she was clearly not a dog for doing the same things three times in a row. She liked to do things once, then move on. I wish, looking back now that also my trainers could have seen that. It would have saved a lot of unnecessary upset, for me mainly, and frustration for Roxy. Because although Roxy was extremely bright and knew exactly how to do each obstacle, we were training in a horse arena, and for her, the best thing about agility was running off and eating as much horse poo as she possible could, before being caught by someone.

This became a weekly event. It wasn't so much agility for the dogs as it was for all the humans chasing Roxy around the hall trying to catch her. I still have no idea to this day why I persevered in taking her.

The Arrival of Tyler 2007

A year and a few months into owning our wonderful little princess, our breeder called us up to explain that Roxys littermate was being rehomed and were we interested in seeing him? We had hoped in a few years to obtain another puppy from our breeder, but we thought he was definitely worth seeing. When we went to meet him, I remember thinking "Wow! He is a beast!" He was much larger than Roxy with a big head and droopy eyes. Roxy was just excited to see her mum and dad again and didn't pay much attention to him. But something obviously clicked, as we took him home that night.

We took him straight down to our local field and let the dogs have a good run around, Ty desperately tried to catch Roxy but due to his unfitness ended up getting a bit stressed out and foaming at the mouth. I did email the breeder to find out if that was normal, and apparently for him that was! So we took them inside where he downed a bowl of water and then promptly wee'd it straight back out onto the lounge floor. He then took his place in the cat's bed and fell asleep. We could tell he was going to fit right in.

Tyler (right) joins us in 2007

This is my bed!

So something we noticed very quickly, and I know we are not the only couple with two dogs who fight over an identical bed, but even to this day, Tyler falls for this trick every single time. It used to happen more so when they were on the sofas but even with their beds on the floor Roxy will still do this, it's a good one. You know it's coming because she will walk past, look at Ty fast asleep in his pure comfort, snoring away, she will carry on walking towards the front door and bark, just once, but it's always enough to wake Tyler up and send him into a frenzy charging towards the front door in a mad panic of being caught off his duty. It gives Roxy more than enough time to slowly walk back towards the seating area, choose her favourite spot on the bed or sofa and curl up before Ty has realised there is nothing to bark at and he has once again been played by Roxy out of his comfy bed.

Roxy laying on Tyler

Mystery of the missing socks

Roxy had been left the entire house since she was a small pup. I recall when she was only about 4 or 5 months old we attempted to shut her in our bedroom to go out for a meal only to come home to a disaster zone. It's amazing how much damage a small innocent puppy can actually achieve.

And although everyone told me to crate her, we actually did the exact opposite and it worked out well for us, which is funny because now I sit there and tell people to crate their dogs who are destroying homes. In Roxy's case, she just didn't like to be confined, and to be honest, every dog is different. You have to know your dog before making a decision like that whether to trust them enough to roam around your house. Anyway as Roxy was used to being left the entire house, we just assumed Ty would also be.

However it didn't take long for us to notice that we were quickly running out of socks. Maybe our washing machine had been stealing more socks than normal? However Ty is not a subtle dog, and one sunny afternoon proudly walked out of our bedroom, with half a chewed sock hanging out of his mouth. As I leant in close to see what he had it was promptly swallowed whole. His obsession became so bad that even if a nephew popped over for a visit and kicked off their socks, Ty would sweep in casually and hoover them up. Baby socks were also a prime target as these were kicked off frequently, so I ended up having to warn guests who came over with small ones, to watch their socks!

The Dustbin

In addition to random sock eating, Ty was also partial to pretty much anything that was in the kitchen bin, mostly the chicken bones from KFC buckets, cat food pouches, leftovers etc. We had to start being very strict about making sure the bin was up out of the way of the dogs before leaving the house. However Laurence wasn't as good as remembering as I was, and after the tenth time of coming home to the litter strewn out throughout the house, he went out and returned home with an expensive Branbantia bin and laundry bin with heavy lids.

The weirdest thing was, even though the bin didn't have a pet lock on it as such and was just a push touch bin, Ty never worked it out, the bin was never touched again after that. Success!

The bin thieves

Thanks for the sandwich

Having given Ty some time to settle in, he clearly felt as if he was in heaven. Who could blame him, free socks and KFC most days, lucky boy. However he stepped over the mark of politeness when one morning, having awoken late for work, I was quickly throwing together a cheese sandwich for my lunch. I had got about as far as putting the bread on the chopping board before desperately needing the toilet.

Having done the 'wee dance' for a while I decided I couldn't hold it anymore and ran to the bathroom. Breathing a sigh of relief, I looked towards the open door in front of me, only to witness Tyler waltzing past the bathroom door, with said cheese sandwich in his mouth, giving me a sideways glance before dropping it to the floor and consuming it whole. Nothing I could do being stuck to the toilet. From then I knew this dog was going to be a sod.

Tyler

Something's at the door

So during this period of our lives Laurence was still working nights. Often I would allow Roxy and Tyler to sleep on the bed with me for company. One night around 2am I awoke to the sight of both Roxy and Tyler sat bolt upright at the end of the bed growling at the closed bedroom door. As I turned on the light they both jumped off the bed, went right up to the bedroom door and started to growl even louder, suddenly I heard a thump come from downstairs. I shushed the dogs and put my ear up to the bedroom door, the thump came again, like someone was falling slowly down the stairs. A million things went through my mind, but I decided to open the door and let the dogs investigate for me.

I called out "I'm coming out, with the dogs!! Leave now!!". I opened the bedroom door and quickly flicked on the landing light as the dogs charged down the stairs. As I neared the top of the stairs, the thumping becoming more apparent and louder, like someone was trying to break in through our front door, the dogs came bounding back up the stairs, tails wagging and looking very pleased with themselves. The banging continued as they went back off to bed, so I walked downstairs alone, only to see next door's poor cat frantically throwing himself at the cat flap to get back OUT of the house. It seemed that I had locked the cat flap to stop our cat going out, I hadn't banked on other cats coming into the property. Lesson learnt.

The Dog Warden

We arrived home one night after work to a note from the dog warden, wanting to speak to us regarding 'Barking Dogs'. This was the first we had heard of our dogs barking when being left during the day. We always left the radio on and hired a dog walker every day. So this came as a bit of a shock to us.

We invited the warden over for a visit. He was pleasantly surprised when he came into our maisonette. Two well behaved, now fully grown Dobermanns, laid down sucking on their blankets. I will always recall when he first sat down him saying "This wasn't what I was expecting at all." I am not sure what he was told or who had said what, but he could clearly see this was a case of neighbourhood gossiping regarding two 'out of control' dogs. He asked us just to record the dogs activity during the day and find out if and when they were barking.

So Laurence, being the technical one, set up a recording device from the computer to cover the lounge and we carried on our days as normal. We discovered quickly that the dogs barked when the postman arrived, when the dog walker arrived and then again when we arrived home. They would also bark if our neighbours decided to stand outside our windows and have very loud conversations.

Regardless, the evidence showed this was normal dog behaviour and not continuous or excessive barking. The dog warden dismissed the case, only for a few more weeks to go past and another complaint to be made, this time directly to the council. Again the dog warden asked the person complaining to keep a diary and get back to him, we never did hear any more about it. We still to this day have no idea why, whoever wanted to make our lives hell, didn't just come to us first and let us know our dogs were barking. We assumed at the time we were good friends with our immediate neighbours. But we were clearly mistaken, shortly after this we became the outcast of the entire village, maybe for having Dobermanns? I am not sure, but it certainly felt that way.

We moved shortly after this.

Tyler and Roxy enjoying a walk 2008

Dog Walking

Unfortunately, or some may say, fortunately, before our move out of the village from hell, I lost my job due to mass redundancies - thanks to the recession of 2008. It was then I had decided my dog walker was making far too much money out of us and that was clearly the business to be in. I am very lucky to have a supporting husband and I couldn't wait to spend all my waking hours walking, looking after and playing with dogs. As with any new business, it took a few years to get off the ground and I could probably write a whole other book on the shenanigans that my clients' dogs got up to in the 5 years I owned "Chilled Dogs". But we'll see how this book does first. Needless to say the twins loved me being home every day, and getting to come out on lots of walks with lots of new playmates. Although I did quickly notice how breedist they were.

This was especially true when we had a Boxer and Dobermann friend come to stay with us for the weekend. It didn't take long before I noticed the three Dobermanns all curled up on one side of the lounge and one poor Boxer sat on his own on the other side. The funniest part was the Dobermann and Boxer who were staying, lived together and spent all day together, yet even this Dobermann has realised what group he was a part of and stuck to the twins like glue.

It didn't take long for Roxy and Ty to work out which clients they liked and which clients they would tolerate.
But for me it was just about spending time with all of them and there nothing better than seeing dogs be free and walking as a pack. I was lucky enough to also have a handful of people help out when the

business grew, and over the summer holidays my nephews would often come and work with me. One of my nephews was eager to learn, had a passion for dogs and would quickly tire the clients out for me! The other simply made me laugh. Whilst he was walking a small and slow Dachshund, he remarked "So far, of the dog walking my favourite dog is this one. Because he is very slow, very small and I love sausages"

The famous Chilled Dogs van 2008

Me walking some clients

What is THAT?

By now you should be aware that Ty does have a habit of eating pretty much anything, but what follows was a new low, even for him.

So around my town there are plenty of bridleways, footpaths, byways to walk your dogs along. However, some people like to trash these walks with various rubbish, I've pretty much seen it all, from tyres, cement, paint, food, a deer's head in a black bag, guns, a policeman's wallet to tampons and nappies. Fortunately no dead bodies! Which is great because you always hear in the news "Dog Walker finds dead body" and I knew one day that could possibly happen to me, but no, I was very lucky and although apparently a murder did occur on one of my walks, I never happened to stumble across a corpse.

Anyway back to the story, on this particular walk, it was quite clear someone couldn't have waited, the vile substance in question was clearly surrounded by toilet paper, and lets just say had a smell that no wildlife could produce. On this walk I had with me two Boxers, Roxy and Ty a Weimeraner and a Pointer. I noticed the boxer had decided to grab some big white bag type thing, so I went over to her to examine further only to find a used tampax hanging out of her mouth, as I was cringing, desperately trying to get her to leave it, to my horror Ty was behind me eating said human faeces. So I then had to run over to him, only for him to jump back, run round me and smear said faeces all down my trouser leg.

Now, I have a seriously bad gag reflex, which kicked in automatically, to which I then had six dogs all pouncing on me! Needless to say I quickly put all the dogs back in the van, threw a bottle of water down my self, wrapped myself in a towel headed home and sat fully dressed under a hot shower. I then put Ty in the shower and if I could have cleaned his mouth out with soap, I would have!

Laurence and Tyler

Here Ya Go Friends

So now more than ever was a time to clamp down on Ty's "leave it" command. We went back to Roxy's puppy trainer to put Ty through his Kennel Club certificates. Ty did fairly well in this class, it was obvious he was more interested in the food reward than what he was actually doing, but he would try his hardest and I had to cut him some slack as he clearly hadn't done this as a puppy.

I remember one evening in our training class, to mix it up a bit, we put all the dogs to the sides of the hall and placed high value exciting toys, treats, balls, furry things in a pile in the middle of the classroom.

The point was to be that we would walk round these items commanding our dogs to 'leave it' and rewarding them for looking the other way. All the while getting closer and closer to the items. I was a little nervous as I thought Ty would struggle with this task, but amazingly he was really good at it, I mean really really good, like he didn't even look once at the exciting things in the middle of the room. It was almost too easy.

But as we were at the finishing line, so very close to all the objects, Ty had obviously clocked a pot of delicious treats within his grasp. As we walked past the pot, without even looking, Ty launched his leg out sideways, smacked this pot of treats so hard they flung across the entire room sending all the other dogs into a frenzy to all hoover up the treats as fast as possible.

I have to hand it to him, he didn't even try to eat any of the treats, he sat politely in front of me, full focus on me. I should disapprove but the whole situation was hilarious - witnessing all these women with their well-behaved, non-challenging Labradors, getting tangled up in each other - the dogs had a blast!

Training with the twins

The 'Top Trainer' number 1!

A little while after Ty's arrival we noticed another behavioural problem, (other than being a food thief) he had started to become obsessed with chasing Roxy and when he did eventually catch her, it would end up in a rough play that neither of them would back down from, no matter where we were, no matter who they ran into and it was getting a little out of hand.

So we decided to call in expert help. This chap came as a recommendation from a forum I believe, anyway he arrived on a Saturday with his wife, and both seemed pleasant. We were quickly put on the spot, asking Roxy and Ty to relinquish their beloved 'sucky pillows' (explanation on Page 71) something we had not done before, but both spat them out when asked.

Then we went for a walk and were both told off for using too many commands and not walking the dogs on the correct side. Then we went up to the field where most of the problems happen but the dogs were never allowed off the lead, instead we did some long lead work, to which Ty of course didn't show any signs of bad behaviour as he knew he was still on lead! 150 quid later, we were told what can only be described as an easy fix - don't let him off the lead. Disappointing day.

The 'Top Trainer' number 2!

So whilst we continued training the twins, we found a new class on a Saturday where Laurence and I could train both of the dogs at the same time. Initially we thought that was an excellent idea, although quickly realised it was stupid. If the twins were in the same class they just wanted to mess about together, but if we worked in separate fields then they would lunge and cry to get back to eachother. How quickly dogs can form a bond in 1 year.

So in comes top trainer number 2! We paid for yet another 1-2-1 to try and tackle Roxy and Ty's obsessive play. But this time I was smart, we wern't about to have another person just watch the dogs on-lead and tell us there is no problem.

So I immediately took both dogs off the lead and very quickly the behaviour started right in front of the trainer! Great! I thought, he is definitely going to do something amazing and magically get them to stop without even having to touch them !!

But no, no, instead all I got was "Can you get them to stop doing that please?!?"

Seriously, SERIOUSLY?! Why did he think we were there, if we could get them to stop we wouldn't need his help in the first place. So I stared at him blankly and said: "That's kind of the point, we can't stop them."He edged towards the field gate, in a desperate attempt to get the hell out of there, like two raging bull's were running savagely across the field towards him and he had no idea what to do.

I felt like I was about to break down into tears. Another wasted session on a trainer that couldn't help us. What felt like hours later, Laurence and I managed to catch the raging bull-dobermanns and we never went back to that training place again.

Roxy and Tyler the fighting lions

Tyler and the cat

One afternoon I had a quiet day, and decided to catch up on some paperwork. After a few moments I could hear a faint high pitched whine coming from upstairs in the bedroom. I listened intently and again, a crying sound. I looked around the room, Roxy was sat next to me on her bed, no sign of Tyler. So I cautiously went upstairs following this whining sound, getting a little concerned, I called out "Ty?" nothing, just another faint whine. As I reached the top of the stairs I peered into the bedroom to see Ty curled up on our bed whining and looking extremely upset, "Whats up mate?" I asked as I walked over towards him. It became apparent the closer I got as to what the problem was. He was upset because the cat had decided to curl up next to him. She on the other hand looked very happy with herself and was using him as her personal massage pillow.

Tyler and Jaffa

Ty joins agility

So against my better judgement, and the fact I was getting nowhere with Roxy I decided to alternate and start taking Ty to agility. We noticed he had one thing in common with his sister and that was running off to eat as much horse poo as he could physically get in his mouth before getting caught by someone. But he did appear to be much more trainable. With Ty he does desperately want to please his handler. Roxy will tolerate her handler until a better offer comes along. Ty would work with anyone, and work well, whereas Roxy would run back to me if someone even spoke to her. It paid off to work with Ty, and as the weeks went on, I ended up dropping Roxy from the class.

Tyler

Roxy goes back to obedience

Whilst feeling guilty for taking Tyler to agility, I entered Roxy into a new type of training called Rally-O. It is effectively an obedience class with different commands at different stations. It was very apparent from the first class she was way too advanced for this, she acted like she'd been there, done it from the very first lesson. Almost like taking a teenager back to playzone, it's fun, but they are certainly not learning anything new.

On the flip side it was in a hall, so no horse poo and she did start to behave much better. To be honest, for once it was nice being told how well-behaved and smart our dog was rather than having a bunch of strangers screaming at her and chasing her down each week.

Roxy winning a demo show

Ty and the stoat

Once in a while something happens that truly bring a smile to your face, for me this was that day, whilst out just me and the twins. We went to the local farmer's field, however, the farmer had just cut down all his crop so the twins were more excited than ever, running up and down the tractor tracks. As Tyler was prancing around, a sudden high pitched 'squeek' came from the field. He stopped suddenly and started to track. I ran over to also see what was making this awful racket. Ty and Roxy were sniffing around when Ty suddenly stopped, poked his nose in the straw, and another squeek came out. Suddenly a little baby stoat popped its head out of the grass and screeched at Ty, I could see there were two hiding under the cut down straw. Ty seemed to understand this stoat's warning and stood very still. Slowly he reached his head down to get a better sniff at this weird looking creature. Roxy by this point was bored and had bounded off to go and roll in some fox poo.

As Ty leant ever so slowly into this creature, lowering his whole front body so he was level with it, the stoat promptly bit his nose. Ty yelped, went into a play bow, and chased the stoat across the field, as they got to one point the stoat stopped, stood upright, squarked at him and then promptly chased Ty back across the field the other way. The whole time Ty was play bowing, wagging his tail and having a blast. I don't know if the stoat felt the same way, but I didn't want to stress the poor creature out anymore, so after I stopped laughing hysterically Ty said his goodbyes and we walked home.

Ty is reunited with his stoat friend

So after going home and bragging to all our friends about how Ty was playing so nicely with a baby stoat, I decided to show them the next day. We set off on our walk down to the local field and we scoured the whole field, no stoat. I then asked Ty to 'find him' which was funny because Ty has no tracking experience and probably had no idea what I was on about, but remarkably he did put his nose to the floor and start sniffing.

Only a few minutes passed when Ty stopped in his tracks and glared at the floor "He's found him!" exclaimed a friend, and we all ran over to see. Unfortunately it seemed so had a bird of prey, and poor little stoat was laying dead with a puncture wound in his chest. What happened next truly bought a tear to my eye, Ty looked so concerned, he very slowly lowered his whole body again and came in close to his stoat friend. As he got further and further down, practically in a laying down position, all of us emotional and sad, he had lost his friend. He ever so slowly, proceeded to roll over him. Gross.

R.I.P Stoat friend

I can work that out

So most people who own dogs would have purchased or at least heard of a treat ball. It is a medium sized hard yellow ball that when rolled around, dispenses a treat for dogs. The point is the dogs use their intelligence to roll the ball and receive the treats. Well I found an even better device whilst in training to be a clicker instructor, I remember it was in a huge hall, and I think I only purchased it to make the instructor like me as I was spending more money on her course.

Anyway, it was a large purple plastic bottle, with a rope coming out of the top. You twisted the bottom to put treats in, but the dogs had to work out that in order to get the treats out you push the rope down which allowed enough gap for a treat to come out the top. The first night I used this was when taking Roxy to Rally-O, I thought it would keep Ty entertained for the evening.

Whilst Roxy was waiting in the car, I gave Ty the bottle and sorted out all my bits I needed for the evening. He banged it around a bit on the floor, it kept slipping from under his paws on our tile flooring and I could see he was getting frustrated with the device. I couldn't have imagined what he did next though. He grabbed the bottle and ran up the stairs. As I observed from downstairs, I suddenly encountered a purple plastic bottle being flung down the stairs and smashing on the floor below me. Ty hurried down, hoovered up the treats and looked at me for another go.

The Landrover

Around 2009 Laurence decided to buy me a Landrover for my business, due to the fact on snow days I was struggling to get out to my clients. This quickly turned into Laurence's new hobby, slowly converting it into an off-roader to take up to Salisbury Plains to enjoy the mud and hills.

The twins loved coming out, they wern't so keen on the odd occasion we'd get stuck in a puddle and the car would flood. But overall it was great to be out with friends and family with all their dogs and let them all run free in the English countryside.

After a few trips out we noticed that Roxy loved running around and being free so much she had decided no longer to go back in the Landrover when called. We often took bribes, so as not to have everyone waiting on us. However one particular trip we forgot our bribes and she knew it! So she bounded off, Laurence, in frustration, said "Fine, if she wants to stay here, then let's get in the car and leave her, she'll panic and come running back" I agreed with the plan as I had read that it can be a good training technique. So we said our goodbyes to Roxy and got in the landy. She stood behind a bush and glared at us.

Laurence slowly started to drive away, and sure enough, she came charging over in a panicked state. But just as we stopped, she ran off again!! So we drove on a bit more, she came running back and ran happily alongside the car like a wild deer, it was beautiful, but again when we stopped she ran off. Then we realised we were just a part in her new game she had invented for herself - running alongside the car.

She loved that game!

Roxy and Tyler in the Landy

Finding a rented property

After renting a family members property for a year with the Twins, and living the quiet life, we decided to rent somewhere instead of buying a house again, but we quickly found it was much more difficult than we ever could have expected. We did however find the perfect house - nice big enclosed garden, parking for several cars, detached and in the country side. So I asked if the landlord accepted pets,

"What kind of pets?"
"Two dogs"
"What breed of dogs would that be?"
"Two Dobermanns"
"OK I will ask"
"OK can you also tell the landlord I am a dog trainer, both our dogs are very obedient, well socialised, short haired and adults who have never chewed any woodwork in a house"
"Yes ok I will pass on the information"

The next morning she called back, I was excited, this was the perfect house!

"Hello Miss Carter. I'm very sorry to say that the landlord will only accept family pet dogs, not Dobermanns"
Pause...
"Excuse me?"

I was too stunned to really have an argument with the letting agent, and to be honest it wasn't her fault. But I was totally and utterly shocked by this comment.

I often hear of people dumping their dogs in rescue because they are moving and can't take the dogs with them, and I've always been disgusted by this "Why on earth can't they find somewhere that will allow dogs?"

Now I'm starting to wonder what **breed** of dogs are being put into rescue due to the ignorance of landlords out there. And it wouldn't surprise me to hear that they are probably, Rottweilers, German Shepherds, Staffordshire Bull Terriers and the like. Surely if landlords accept 'family pets' then they should ask to meet the dogs if they are unsure, see how they are in a home environment, maybe even get written references for dogs.

Seriously people, let's not damn those dogs who are trained, obedient and loving family pets just because of their breed.

Twins 2010

The Apple Tree

I am pleased to tell you we did finally find a house to move into. However this property came with a huge apple tree, which as you can guess Ty fell in love with and wouldn't leave this tree alone. So let me set the day up for you. Lots of silly mistakes by me, bedroom door left open, came home to four chewed up socks. An afternoon of lounging in the sun also led to pinching sticks around the garden and chewing them up, then an evening wee consisted of also going out to find any apples that may have been knocked off the tree by the wind, several devoured.

The first night we had a few moments pacing, a few times sick, myself not awake enough to work out what was going on. The second night, similar thing, but I awoke just as Ty was licking the carpet clean. The third night Ty was sick, I vaguely saw what looked like a black slipper on the floor only to be hoovered up by Ty again. So by the fourth night, I'd had enough, Ty was sick, I flicked the light on, ran over, just as he was hoovering it back up, I shoved my hand down his throat and pulled out what I can only describe to be the most vile smelling obstacle I had ever held in my bare hands. A foot long mixture of socks, sticks, rope bit and entire crab apples. How that boy does it is beyond me.

Vegetarian Dobermanns

So when the twins wern't helping themselves to the apple tree, they discovered a whole new type of food, again, completely my fault. We were out blackberry picking one sunny morning to put the berries on our apple crumble we were making later that day.

After making the crumble, we had a few berries left over and after briefly researching whether or not a dog is allowed to eat a blackberry I offered the remainders to Roxy and Ty. I never in my wildest dreams imagined that in the following weeks they would scour out every blackberry bush on our walks, stop and help themselves to the blackberries, although what was more interesting was the precision they used to not get pricked by the thorns and how they would avoid the red ones that wern't ripe and only pick the best juicy ones.

This would be an extremely useful skill if I could also get them to bag them up for me!

Roxy eating Blackberries

The Swimming

Well, the agility season was over and I had heard of a new canine hydrotherapy pool opening up locally. I was very excited about taking the twins, who were now both 6 years old, down there to swim and thought it would be a great way to keep them in shape over the winter whilst it was too cold to go out and train. So we went down to meet the crew and to sign up. For the first swim, Ty went first, he was fitted up with a life jacket, and slowly lead down the ramp to the water.

Ty wasn't impressed and unfortunately the ramp didn't go down far enough for him to even attempt to get his belly wet, so the trainer had to lift Ty up and lower him into the water manually. Ty clung to him like a cat being put into water, even the trainer was in hysterics, as even when Ty was in the water he was still holding onto this poor bloke for dear life. Eventually Ty let go and spotted a ball to play with, so promptly swam off and got the hang of it!

Roxy was a very different story. Having been mortified by having to wear a life jacket. She wouldn't even go down the ramp after spotting what was at the end of it. So again she was lifted in manually but whilst bobbing around in her life jacket she lifted up all 4 paws and tucked them under herself and outright refused to swim.

We attended this swimming facility for 2 more years, and I can tell you after two years, she still bobbed around that pool whilst tucking her legs up!!! At least I know now that if she ever did seriously need hydrotherapy then it's almost pointless making her try to swim.

However after 2 years with Ty, I now have a dog who loves to jump into water after a ball and gets good exercise.

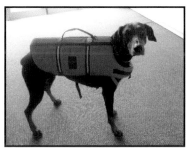

Roxy not approving of her lifejacket

Ty loving it

Roxy tolerating it

The Ice-cream

Now you're probably thinking, why, oh why, would I do this with everything else you've read so far in this book. Well, lets just say I had memory loss for the sake of saving my reputation. It was a hot sunny day in the van, but fortunately a short working day so I treated myself to a lovely ice-cream on the way home from work.

As I walked through the door, the twins greeted me in their usual overly excited manor, then they both paused and glared at the vision of beauty in my hand.. the ice-cream.

I've often seen people share their ice-cream with their dogs and thought it was gross to be honest, but Roxy looked so cute, I thought I'd let her have just one lick. And she did, and seemed very pleased with herself. I then looked at Tyler who was giving me those same puppy dog eyes. I couldn't resist... I held out the ice-cream.. Chomp... I was left with an inch of cone!

Tyler

Competing in Agility

After being part of our local agility club for many years, it finally occurred to me we wern't actually getting anywhere. We'd started in the beginners group and never actually progressed. I am pretty sure this is down to the fact that I didn't own a Collie and therefore could not help represent the club - I was not one of the best examples of clientele. That, and every now and again people still had to stop and chase Ty around the horse arena when he was bored and went off on a poo hunt. But under the influence of my fellow club members I started competing with Tyler and doing fairly well actually, OK we were never the fastest, but he was a very dedicated competitor and he always tried his hardest, no matter how much I messed up.

However I won't lie to you and tell you he never put a paw wrong. If food was involved he became impossible to handle. This became apparent on one of our first shows where just at the start/finish line, (entrance to the hall) a very intelligent individual decided of all the places, that was an excellent place to display all his produce, for dogs, including pigs ears, rawhides, dog food, toys, leads, you name it - Ty's happy place.

As we went into the hall to line up, I caught Ty having a good old sniff on his way past, desperately trying to gain his focus back onto me I did what any other hopeless person would do in this situation and lined my fingernails with cheese! As it was our turn to run, the cheese appeared to be working, he was looking at me and listening to commands, yes, wohoo! It's going great! A few mishaps on the way round but he rushed towards the finish line, and for one very good reason of course. He promptly ran out of the hall over to the dog food stand, grabbed an entire bag of pigs ears and buggered off into the car park.

Tyler too tired to pose

Bounding through the weaves

The Tracking

So back to the drawing board. What else would the twins enjoy? It's never too late to change the sport. What would be Ty's ideal job? I pondered. Then it struck me, he could sniff out a breadcrumb in a haystack, I needed to find a local working trials club! We were fortunate to find a trainer within about an hour's drive who was happy to set up a class for just our needs. Although he covered most of the working trials skill sets, we were only really interested in the tracking part.

The twins both picked up tracking footsteps really quickly. Much to my amazement Roxy picked it up much faster, although in hindsight it was obvious the reason why, Tyler is so food obsessed that when the food pieces were not placed in the tracking footsteps he didn't really want to play anymore. So it took him a little longer to work out the point of the exercise, and that it wasn't just 'find the sausage in the grass' training.

Although both dogs excelled in tracking it was short lived due to the inconsistency in members actually showing up. However I do remember vividly meeting one such member, a Dobermann breeder who thought she was obviously very important, and irritated that I had no idea who she was. If there's one thing I dislike about some breeders is their absolute disdain for other breeders. Henceforth, once this woman found out that the twins had a certain kennel name in their line, she immediately starting pointing out their flaws. "Oh yes well THAT line is known for producing wonky dogs, look at your boys walk, he can't walk properly, and look at the state of your girls ears, they are mangled, that is a breeding problem"

I found the whole situation highly ironic when she produced her top show dog, that was highly dog-aggressive, so much so, we all had to put our dogs away whilst he trained. Oh yes of course, THAT'S the best thing to breed from, let's put more aggression into the breed, that's what we need, damn those wonky eared good-natured Dobermanns!

Laurence tracking with Ty

Me and Roxy

Cuddles with Ty

The Tissue

Whilst out on a rare sunny and warm walk with the twins one afternoon I realized I had a few treats left in my pocket from some puppy training I had been doing that morning. So I did a few recalls with Roxy and Ty just to re-inforce the behaviour and then carried on my way. However Ty would not stop bugging me after that, nosing my pocket, running away a bit then running straight back as if to say "Look mum, I'm still doing it where's my treat??" To which point to prove the non-existence of treats in my pocket I turned them inside out, there was a tissue in there, I held it out to show him there was no more treats - and he promptly swallowed the tissue whole and trotted off on his merry way....

Tyler

The 'Top Agility Trainer'

Well after being bugged profusely by my good friend, I decided, after all these years to go and see yet another agility trainer. This one, as my friend had stated, was apparently absolutely fantastic with the more 'challenging' types of dogs. So I arrived, not in the right frame of mind. To be honest I had almost given up with agility as a whole, so when faced with the question "Why are you here, what do you want?" All I managed to respond with was "My friend made me come here."Good start.

After a short discussion, I quickly realised I wasn't going to be her best friend. She was obviously a very high-level competitor, and I was a dog lover who just wanted to have a bit of fun.

Anyway seeing as I was paying a high fee for her one-to-one attention, I decided to make the most of it and show off the dogs a bit. Roxy completely impressed me, her drive round the agility course just to a tennis ball was amazing, she was focused, concentrating, LISTENING to me. This was not the same dog! So I was really overwhelmed with pride, a tear in my eye, when my bubble was quickly burst by a

"Don't let her do that!"

Oh ok, she had a little sniff to the floor, no big deal, so I got her focus for a short while but then she went to go and sniff the floor again, then those fatal words came out of the trainer's mouth "That is unacceptable, tell her she can't do that"

Hmmm... Tell her she can't do that??..... I'VE BEEN TRYING FOR 6 SODDING YEARS if you have some kind of magic trick that I have never tried or done then PLEASE let me know what that is! I could hang a flipping steak round my neck and Roxy would still be more interested in the floor than myself!!!

Anyway bar that little incident, and then, well honestly, several more in the eyes of the trainer, I think both the dogs did really well. So after pondering on my thoughts for a little while, and being told on my way out that I shouldn't really be competing in the agility field. I decided to completely ignore that and continue competing - just to enjoy agility and make it fun for my dogs.

Agility, shouldn't this be fun?

Roxy the little mischief!

The Rain

Our very next agility event happened to fall on a day when it was raining, which to be fair, in the UK, isn't unusual. However this was the first show we'd attended where the rain was belting down sideways, and even stood in the queue Ty was desperately trying to stand behind me and shelter himself as much as possible from the rain. He wasn't a happy boy.

But we were up next, and I managed to get Ty out into a good position on the starting line, I walked on ahead ready to start the course, and then I called two or three times "Ty come on, go!!" but he sat there shivering with his eyes shut, rain blasting against his poor little face. Maybe he just couldn't hear me over the blustering winds? So I started to walk back and called again, "Ty... Go!!"He clocked me, stood upright and ran... and ran.... to the nearest tree for shelter!!! What little audience remained around the course lines, all burst into laughter, even the judge was trying hard to cover her smiles. I think I must own the biggest wimp on the agility field...

Tyler doesn't like the rain

Celebrity Dobermann!

So after watching my yearly crufts fix, a little advert popped up for a new pet modelling website. I have absolutely no idea what prompted me to sign up, even after being stung with a joining up fee I still gave it a go. Unsurprisingly we never got a call. However after my years subscription had ended, we did get a call, seems one photographer was looking for a Dobermann that didn't have a tail and Ty fitted the bill. The agency gave me two days notice and informed me it would be a calendar photoshoot for a male celebrity. So I spoke to Laurence that night and asked if he could get the Monday off work and come to London with me to attend the photoshoot. He said no. Then the agency called again to inform me it was a female celebrity, so I asked him again. We joked that it would be for a z list celebrity and besides how would he explain getting the day off at such short notice to his boss. So I asked my good friend who also had good knowledge of pet modelling as her Jack Russell was currently the face of PetLog. She agreed, I asked all my clients nicely for the afternoon off and we both headed up to the centre of London to meet this mysterious female celebrity.

As we waited in an old museum loft, we both couldn't help but think that actually we had been set up and we were about to become part of some sick TV prank. We were surrounded with wigs and no one else was there. An hour or so later, a lady in a robe walked in, followed by one man.

I couldn't believe my eyes, it was Cheryl Cole! One of the most popular singers in the UK at that time and she was a judge on X-factor. Before I could speak she took one look at Tyler and ran over for a cuddle. It turned out the man behind her was her brother, who was a really nice guy who kept my friend and me company for the day. It took every ounce of my body not to text Laurence to announce that the lady who was standing in front of me was someone, who at the time, he had a huge celebrity crush on! Anyway moving on, Ty was having the time of his life, snuggled up to Cheryl.

It only got better for Ty as an entourage of about 10-15 people turned up, and promptly set up a huge buffet. Everyone wanted to feed the dog who was crying and pining at the end of the buffet table. It was probably so unprofessional, but hey, I'd never seen Ty eat a meringue either and it seemed to entertain everyone.

We waited a while longer for Cheryl to have her make-up done, and then went through for our photoshoot. It was pretty simple, she was in a chair whilst Ty stood in a doorway behind her. So I put Ty in his stay and stood behind the photographer. Everyone in the room was so proud of Ty for standing there so well-behaved and had his full focus on me. I have to admit, I was also pleased it was all going well, I'd never done anything like this before. Then it was actually Cheryl's idea to have Ty come and sit up next to her in the photo. So I put Ty in a sit and again stood behind the photographer. She kept patting him and giving him fuss and getting him to give her kisses, which made me laugh hysterically but annoyed her make up artists. Anyway, the final photo was lovely, and Tyler made the 2013 Calendar under April. I am not sure if for copyright reasons I am allowed to put the photo in this book, but I am sure if you enter Cheryl Cole Dobermann into the internet you will see our handsome boy proudly sitting with Cheryl. He was featured centre-spread of a national news-paper and for a laugh we even set him up with his very own Facebook Page. I also stupidly decided to give an interview to Nick Grimshaw of Radio 1 to explain why my dog tried to sit on Cheryl Cole's face (unsurprisingly that was the only sentence they picked up on). Well - ride off the back of your dogs fame and all that...

Ty and the Rabbit

I have always been worried for rabbits in our garden with Ty around. Although I have not mentioned it in this book, when he was younger he did manage to catch a rabbit with myxomatosis, and whilst in play with another dog ended up killing it (it did cause a bit of panic over the safety of our cat for a few weeks) however since then he has been known to play nicely with small animals ie the stoat previously mentioned. This particular afternoon it was warm and sunny, a rarity in England, so the back door was left open and I was in and out pottering around the house.

After a while of pottering, I noticed Ty had been stood in one place fixated on something in the flower beds for quite a bit of time. So I decided to call over to him to see what he was up to. He ignored me, and tilted his head slightly, lowered his body and crept forward. I was squinting hard to see what on earth he was looking at, and then, a flicker of brown fur, yep there was a massive rabbit in the middle of the flower bed, munching away on all my new sweet-pea seedlings.

Glancing back to Ty I cautiously called him away, but he was fairly close to the rabbit by this point, who again, I can only assume, was riddled with some kind of disease as it wasn't moving from it's munching ground.

But as Ty got close to the rabbit it became apparent he was more interested in what it was actually eating. Ty took his opportunity and swiftly proceeded to eat as many sweet peas as he could get before the rabbit stole this glorious free food from the garden. I swear, if I am not fighting against the wildlife for my flowers to grow, now I am also fighting against the dogs.

Ty watching the rabbit

The culprit

Work days are tiring

Laurence found out in 2012 that he may have the opportunity to work in the USA. Once we knew the move was on for certain I took the decision to sell up my beloved dog walking business and help out some family members by working on a private estate, gardening. The one great thing about this new position was that I could bring the dogs to work with me!

I think I was more excited at this opportunity than the dogs were, to be honest. I decided to be sensible about this new freedom and ensure only one dog at a time was out roaming the 10 acres of land with me, and let's face it, with Tylers track record for eating everything (including sweetpeas) it was mostly Roxy who got to come outside. When it was either too hot or cold, I tried to introduce Roxy and Tyler to the wonderful dog room that the owners had offered to us, heated beds, comfort, in a lovely re-painted barn. Would they settle in there? Like hell they would!

The three or four times I did try them out in the dog room, even from three miles away I could hear Roxy howling! So that quickly made up my mind to just let them stay in the van if they couldn't be out with me. Humourously with Ty we found that if he couldn't find anything to eat on the 10 acres, then he would sulk back off to the van and go back to sleep anyway!

Ty joining me whilst out mowing

The Flying Dobermann

So this was on one of the rare occasions I actually had Ty out for the afternoon whilst I was mowing the top lawns. Ty was being well-behaved for a change and staying close by. I had assumed I was on my own in the estate this particular afternoon, until I heard what sounded like clipping coming from one of the lower lawns.

I walked over slowly to peer over the wall and approximately 3 metres below me I spotted two contract gardeners trimming the front box hedging. My sigh of relief was interrupted by Tyler deciding to jump up onto the wall to also have a look and quickly realising it was too unstable for him to stand on, so he launched himself off the wall and smack bang into the box hedging below. I can't even begin to describe the look on this man's face as an 80lb Dobermann came hurtling at him from out of the sky. Ty made a quick recovery, he stood up, stumbled into and ruined another hedge before trotting off as if nothing had happened. I heard that the gardener was in shock for the rest of the afternoon.

The Bird Food

2013 seemed to be the year to feed the birds at work, it had not regularly happened before but this year the fat filled coconut balls came into play. To be honest I was not aware of this until promptly faced with CCTV footage, from the estate manager, showing a lump of a Dobermann jumping up at some very expensive bird tables and pinching said coconut balls off the feeders and running off with them. Although Roxy wasn't little miss innocent after Ty had dispensed said bird seed everywhere, you see her sneak into the shot and hoover up all the evidence. I have to hand it to them, if they hadn't been caught no one would be any the wiser!

Only a week later I was also informed that Ty had managed to sniff out the brussels sprouts, fought his way into the vegetable patch and ran off with the crops. The twins spent the next few weeks in the van!

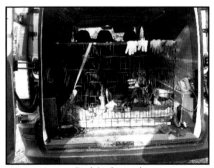

Back in the van!

The Pumpkins

So another halloween, another quiet day at work. Actually this occurred a few days after halloween and unfortunately for me, I didn't spot the family's pumpkins all disposed of in Ty's favourite place to be found at work – the compost bin!

What I did spot however was a Dobermann running at full pelt across the donkey field with a huge Pumpkin in his mouth partly covering his face. He thoroughly enjoyed that one.

Tyler and Roxy at work

The Muzzled Labrador

Now I am more than used to people giving me a wide berth on our dog walks, but this was one of those special moments I won't forget. We were hiking up over the hills of Abbots Ann, a place where I had met a lot of friendly people who didn't run screaming in the other direction at the sight of two large Dobermanns.

However this day, after squeezing through our usual gap in the hedge through to the field, an overweight, yellow Labrador, fully muzzled came tearing over towards us and body slammed Tyler. Ty, in a state of shock had a bit of a grumble and kind of stood his ground. What made this funnier was the owner, a middle-aged lady, came running over the hill exclaiming "Amber!! AMBER!! Come away from those terrible dogs, they will have you for dinner!"Now I am more than used to this with small dog owners and I understand that they obviously fully believe my dog, with a choice of any food in the world would just love to eat their little dog, but a fat Labrador that was twice the size of my dogs, didn't make much sense.

What did she think she owned? In reality she owned a bullying labrador, that she clearly knew had problems as she had muzzled it yet I still get attacked verbally for having the vicious dogs, purely because of their looks. Sigh, some people just never learn.

Discover Dogs

Late 2012, my friend had asked me to accompany her to a dog show in London called Discover Dogs. She needed me to run her agility dog in the rescue demonstration, as she was heavily pregnant at the time. I was happy to oblige, and in turn she gave me a ticket to bring a dog. I had already decided it would be Tyler as Roxy has a habit of shutting down in large groups and God forbid that anyone there was a large man in a wicker hat.

When we arrived there was a lot of waiting around, Ty was good as usual, soaking up all the attention from thousands of passers by and lounging about pretty much anywhere he could. After the demo we decided to take a walk around the stands. One such stand was displaying a new type of contraption to engage your dogs thinking. It was effectively a big fake green grass circle with treats in between the blades. These things were obviously on the floor as a demonstration to show dogs 'working it out', sniffing and using their minds to individually lick out each treat. I don't think this woman had banked on a very food obsessed Dobermann quickly working out the best way to get all the treats at once, which was simply to flip the device over, push it to one side and consume all the treats. Wasn't a great marketing pitch for her.

Well Saved

Now for a nice story, this one is more about myself than the dogs, but I thought at this point I would share with you one of the greatest moments to me as a dog lover. During the summer of 2013 we had my aunt come stay with us for a few days. One morning I popped to the local blood bank to donate as usual, however due to parking restrictions at this particular venue I had opted to skip my usual tea and biscuit afterwards and head home before I got a parking ticket!

When I arrived home I quickly started cooking in the kitchen as my aunty and I were preparing dinner. After a few hours my body obviously realised I needed something as I reached for the can of cold RedBull in the fridge. The music was up loud in the kitchen and the dogs were dancing with us as we were cooking away, but after a few sips I realised something wasn't right. I thought maybe I was going to be sick.

So I left the kitchen, shut the door, headed down the hallway towards the bathroom and unfortunately didn't make it far before collapsing into a heap in the hall. Having slightly come around back to consciousness I couldn't move or barely speak, I was still alone, so I tried hard to call out for help. I could remember briefly hearing the music blaring whilst drifting in and out of a conscious state - I mumbled again for help. Suddenly the dogs began to bark loudly. I knew if I could keep the dogs barking it would eventually anger Laurence enough to come out and see what was going on.

Although he was also home he had to attend a work phone

conference in the study, so he was also shut away. I could hear Roxy start to squeal and Ty's loud barking penetrate through the door and into the hallway. Sure enough, my aunt came out to see what they were barking at and found me on the floor. Shortly after Laurence came out of the study, hilariously still on his phone conference to which I remember hearing the words "Sorry I have to go, my wife has passed out on the floor."

Fortunately after a few minutes and having spoken to my mother-in-law, who is a nurse, we all remembered I was a numpty and had simply forgotten to drink or eat anything after my blood donation. So after a nice cup of tea and a biscuit I was back to my normal self. Lesson learnt, we were all glad it hadn't been anything worse, but for me having the dogs barking and alerting family to my aid was special, and I know they will always look out for me.

Me and the twins 2013

The Twins and the Postman

It's a well known fact that dogs like to bark at the postman. Now our first postie was great, Roxy used to run down and say hello to him in our little flat. But as we moved around we saw less and less of the postman and it soon became a barking match between the two dogs as to who sounded the most threatening to get this intruder to go away. So I naturally just kept the dogs away when retrieving parcels and it became a habit.

One afternoon I was saying goodbye to a dog-boarding client, with the front door wide open. Suddenly Roxy and Tyler leapt out of the front door running and barking, as I looked round I could see the postman stomping up the driveway. Honestly, without hesitation, the postman, who kept striding forward, quickly produced two dog treats from out of his pocket, gave it to the dogs, handed me the post, patted each dog on the head and then left. Even the dogs were in complete shock I think, they just stood there watching him walk away. They never really barked at him again after that!

The Big Move

The twins coped remarkably well whilst over a period of six months Laurence and I were packing up our entire lives and steadily shipping everything to the USA. Alas the moment had come to say goodbye to the twins for just a week, whilst we 'set up shop'. Early Friday morning on the 18th November 2013 we dropped the dogs off with my sister and made our way to the airport. This was one of the hardest journeys of my life, we were leaving behind our family and friends to start this new journey, it was an emotion full of excitement and sadness. But at least I had the comfort that the dogs would only be a week behind us and I knew once we were together again it would help us feel more settled.

When we landed we spent the entire week buying furniture, food, sorting out utility accounts, banks etc. But more importantly buying new dog food, new toys and new dog beds! It flew past so quickly I actually don't think we gave ourselves enough time, but the following Friday, my brother-in-law called to say he was on his way to the airport with the dogs. This had been arranged so that they could be with someone they knew right up to the last minute. We had also organised a great company, who deal with exporting live animals to manage all the paperwork, sort the crates and ferry them to and from the plane so we didn't have to worry about a thing.

At 2am my brother-in-law emailed me a photo just before they were loaded into the crates, Ty was leaning on the cargo staff, typical. Roxy was being fussed by the organiser. They looked happy. I don't think I have ever been in more of a state of panic for their entire journey for them, and knowing them they probably didn't care. What felt like a lifetime later, the twins arrived safe and sound, we rushed to the

Customs' Office to collect them, then slowly opened the sealed crates so as not to be too emotional and worry them. Ty sauntered out like he'd just awoken from a good nap, stretched and had a yawn. Roxy snuck out, head down, ears back, waggling her whole body like we'd just come home from an evening out (which to Roxy feels like a lifetime)

Once we returned home Ty was obviously over the moon to be in a new house. He promptly 'face-slid' across every carpet in the new house and rolled about. However it seemed Roxy had done her 'panic in the lift' scenario and tensed up for the flight, so needless to say she was a bit sore as the night went on, but by the next morning she was back to jumping around and beating up her brother.

Tyler ready to go!

Huge sigh of relief when the twins landed

The French Doors

Now you may be thinking, how have I made it through life NOT being somewhere where they had clear-glass french doors. Well the twins have made it to the age of 8 without experiencing the fun that is a french door. Shortly after the twins had landed in the US of A. Ty was more than excited to be in the new house so that he quickly forgot himself whilst playing out in the garden, and yes you guessed it, ran promptly flat out into the new french doors. But that wasn't the funniest part, the part that couldn't stop us laughing was that Roxy had obviously witnessed this and decided to outright refuse to go through the doors without a paw check first.

Although even with the doors completely wide open she would stand there pawing at it and deciding it couldn't be trusted, so would sit and wait for us to close it and re-open it. It reminded me of a You Tube video where they had taken out a window pane from a front door and the dog wouldn't step through, they even picked this little dog up and put her through the door and she promptly sat the other side waiting to come back in. Well this was our intelligent Dobermann for you. Never trust a door even if your paw goes straight through it!

Roxy checking the door

The Pillows

Now anyone who owns a Dobermann will immediately know exactly what I am on about when we refer to pillow sucking/comfy blanket/duvet comforting. Well there are many terms we all use but in our house it's a 'sucky pillow'. And if you've never seen this extraordinary behaviour in a dog please don't hesitate to google Dobermanns sucking pillows as you will find an abundance of videos of this weird yet wonderful behaviour.

For Ty however this also extends to carrying said pillow around the house with him until I have stopped moving and he can settle down to continue sucking on his pillow. However in our new property we are back to having stairs, something which Ty has not experienced for around 3 or 4 years. And clearly he had forgotten it is not a good idea to try and carry a big pillow in your mouth whilst walking down the stairs. Needless to say this particular morning I ended up with a crumpled Dobermann at the bottom of our stairs, still holding the pillow in his mouth, making a remarkable "that didn't happen" recovery, swiftly got up and trotted off as if nothing had happened or to be spoken of again.

Roxy and Tyler "Pillow sucking" 2013

The Dog Park

So the dog park is a whole new concept to me and the twins. In the UK, dogs are not so restricted and are allowed to walk in many places off the lead. However we found pretty quickly that this was not the case in Virginia. The dogs had to be on-lead in many places, so the only place where they could legally run around off-lead were the dog parks. However these parks are quite small and usually full of lots of other dogs.

Roxy and Tyler have been adjusting pretty well to the new scheme of things and slowly taking advantage of what the dog parks do have to offer. For Roxy this means lots of random people throwing a ball for her and it keeps her entertained for hours. For Ty, on the other hand, this place is full of human attention and food.

Only last week I was busy throwing the tennis ball for Roxy trying to keep her active, when I realised Ty had wandered off. I spotted him over the other side of the park leaning on some poor man who was patting Tyler's head. I carried on playing with Roxy, only this time when I turned round Ty was stood in the middle of a group of about ten women, who were all patting his head and giving him treats. I carried on playing ball with Roxy. The third time I turned around, Ty was fully sat on some poor bloke's lap on a park bench demanding attention. This time I went over and apologised to the bloke squished underneath Ty, but to be honest the chap loved it, as did everyone else, Ty is a very popular dog at the dog park now.

Our new life in the USA has just begun....

ABOUT THE AUTHOR

Natalie has always been a huge animal lover, growing up looking after family pets, including birds, ferrets, cats, chickens, fish, chipmunks, gerbils and, of course, dogs. Natalie began her career in Marketing and IT, but since falling in love with her first dog, Roxy, found that animals, nature and the outdoors was her real passion.

Natalie has over 6 years experience working with dogs. Natalie started her new career path Dog walking & Pet sitting in 2008 and during the following years attended many courses to learn how to train dogs and understand behavioural problems.

Printed by Amazon Italia Logistica S.r.l.
Torrazza Piemonte (TO), Italy